Green
ACTION

Green
ACTION

GREEN ACTION
A New Internationalist BOOK TO GO

Published by New Internationalist Publications Ltd
55 Rectory Road
Oxford OX4 1BW
www.newint.org
New Internationalist is a registered trademark

Cover image by Don Hammond/Corbis.
Credits for other images on Page 190.

© New Internationalist 2005

Designed/Edited by Alan Hughes/Chris Brazier/Adam Ma'anit.

Printed on recycled paper by South China Printing Co Ltd,
Hong Kong, China.

British Library Cataloguing-in-Publication Data.
A catalogue record for this book is available from the British Library.

ISBN 1 904456 22 7

Introduction

BOOKS FILLED WITH inspirational quotes about the environment abound. Even the élite corporate lobby group, the US Chamber of Commerce, has produced a book of green quotations – though not in the interests of promoting a profound love and respect for nature, it has to be said. So why this one?

Well, we felt that the others leave much to be desired, often only selecting the most well-known names – predominantly white men – and paying scant attention to the diversity of the movement fighting for social and ecological harmony.

This book is therefore intended to acknowledge at least some of the countless thousands of extraordinary people doing their part to stop the destruction of the planet. They demonstrate not only that another world is possible, but that it is in the making.

Adam Ma'anit

Today's mighty oak is just yesterday's nut that held its ground.

Anonymous

10

HUMAN BEINGS and the natural world are on a collision course. Human activities inflict harsh and often irreversible damage on the environment and on critical resources. If not checked, many of our current practices put at serious risk the future that we wish for human society... and may so alter the living world that it will be unable to sustain life in the manner that we know. Fundamental changes are urgent if we are to avoid the collision our present course will bring about.

'Warning to Humanity' issued by the Union of Concerned Scientists including a majority of the world's living Nobel Laureates, 1993

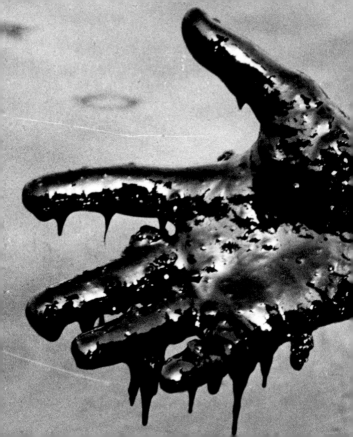

It wasn't the Exxon Valdez captain's driving that caused the Alaskan oil spill. It was YOURS.

Greenpeace advertisement, New York Times, 25 February 1990

14

ORGANIC AGRICULTURE IS THE DEEPEST MOVEMENT FOR PEACE.

Vandana Shiva (1952-),
Indian physicist and
ecologist

The greatness of a nation and its moral progress can be judged by the way its animals are treated.

Mohandas Karamchand Gandhi (1869-1948), leader of India's freedom movement

A WAY OF LIFE THAT EVER MORE RAPIDLY DEPLETES THE POWER OF THE EARTH TO SUSTAIN IT AND PILES UP EVER MORE INSOLUBLE PROBLEMS FOR EACH SUCCEEDING GENERATION CAN ONLY BE CALLED VIOLENT.

Ernst Friedrich Schumacher (1911-1977), German economist and pioneer of appropriate technology

19

TRADITIONALLY, THE INDIGENOUS GROUPS RESPECT THE LAND. NOT PRESERVE — RESPECT. SOCIETY HAS TO PRESERVE WHAT IS LEFT.

Carlos Alberto Ricardo (contemporary), Brazilian
human rights and environmental campaigner

THE WORLD
IS OURS TO
CHANGE —

and if we do not change it, if we do not take up the relentless industrial railroad track and set it running in a new direction, then our descendants will reap a whirlwind that will make most of the events in history hitherto seem small.

Chris Brazier (1955-), English writer

TO ME, THE QUESTION OF THE ENVIRONMENT IS FAR MORE OMINOUS THAN THAT OF PEACE AND WAR. I'M MORE WORRIED ABOUT GLOBAL WARMING THAN I AM ANY MAJOR MILITARY CONFLICT.

Hans Blix (1928-), Swedish, former chief UN weapons inspector in Iraq

25

WE ARE LIVING ON THIS PLANET AS IF WE HAD ANOTHER ONE TO GO TO.

Terri Swearingen (1957-), US health worker and environmentalist

*Water
is the
collective
heritage of
humanity
and nature.
The rains do not
fall on one person's
roof so why should
a few shareholders
appropriate it to line
their pockets? Water
must remain a public good
for the public interest.*

Rudolf Amenga-Etego (contemporary),
Ghanaian lawyer and activist

THE CULTURE OF CAPITAL AND THE CULTURE OF AVARICE HAS FORCED ITSELF UPON NATURE TO ACHIEVE ITS GOALS — NO MATTER WHAT THE SACRIFICE.

Luis Macas (contemporary), Quechuan
indigenous rights activist, Ecuador

Free nature, in my view, can only begin to emerge when we live in a fully participatory society literally free of privilege and domination

Only then will we be able to rid ourselves of the idea of dominating nature and fulfil our promise for acting as a moral, rational, and creative force in natural as well as social evolution.

Murray Bookchin (1921-), US author and founder of the Social Ecology movement

I HAVE HELD IN MY HAND THE GERM OF A PLANT ENGINEERED TO GROW, YIELD ITS CROP, AND THEN MURDER ITS OWN EMBRYOS, AND THERE I GLIMPSED THE MALEVOLENCE THAT CAN LIE IN THE HEART OF A PROFITEERING ENTERPRISE.

Barbara Kingsolver (1955-), US novelist, speaking about 'Terminator Technology' which prevents farmers from saving genetically engineered seeds.

Consumerism is addictive, and like all addictions it involves the denial of its consequences.

Ian G Barbour (contemporary), US physicist and theologian

Trees are poems that earth writes
upon the sky,
We fell them down and turn them
into paper,

That we may record our emptiness.

Kahlil Gibran (1883-1931), Lebanese poet

Student protesters in Tiananmen Square, Beijing.

The highest expression of dignity can be summed up in the single word 'No!' – being able to say 'No!' when you disagree.

Dai Qing (contemporary), Chinese journalist and campaigner against China's Three Gorges Dam project

However fragmented the world, however intense the national rivalries, it is an inexorable fact that we become more interdependent every day. I believe that national sovereignties will shrink in the face of universal interdependence.

The sea, the great unifier, is humanity's only hope. Now, as never before, the old phrase has a literal meaning: We are all in the same boat.

Jacques-Yves Cousteau (1910-1997), French oceanographer

Over the last ten years there has been a changing role between business and NGOs. It is like a dance taking place between the two groups where they are slowly getting closer and closer.

Francis Sullivan (contemporary), Director of Conservation at WWF-UK currently on secondment to British banking giant HSBC, as quoted by Andy Rowell in 'Corporations "Get Engaged" to the Environmental Movement', 2001.

A Malaysian logging company at work in the rainforest, in Gabon, West Africa. The WWF employee is supposed to ensure that loggers stick to the rules and do not hunt wild animals.

45

THE CAR is emblematic of the human enterprise that is killing off so many species today. Many scientists say that 'biological diversity' is declining at a dangerous rate. Meanwhile, the artificial diversity of the machine explodes as we humans repopulate the depleted biosphere with creatures of our own invention... We must look beyond the car into the artificial heart of modern society if we are to save ourselves from an object that is but a projection of our own unsatisfied desires.

Jeremiah Creedon (contemporary), US journalist and cultural commentator

When you give food to the poor, they call you a saint. When you ask why the poor have no food, they call you a communist.

Archbishop Helder Camara (1909-1999), Brazilian liberation theologist

49

OUR FIGHT against incineration, landfills and polluting technologies is actually a struggle against the negative and destructive forces of overconsumption and dirty industrial development. It is essentially a struggle to shift the dominant paradigm to one which is truly respectful of life and the rights of future generations.

Von Hernandez (1966-), activist who helped make the Philippines the first country in the world to ban waste incineration

For one species to mourn the death of another is a new thing under the sun. The Cro–Magnon who slew the last mammoth thought only of steaks. The sportsman who shot the last [Passenger] pigeon thought only of his prowess. The sailor who clubbed the last auk thought of nothing at all.

Aldo Leopold (1887-1948), US ecologist

The forest is not a resource for us, it is life itself. It is the only place for us to live.

Evaristo Nugkuag (contemporary), Peruvian indigenous rights activist

If we do not change our direction, we are likely to end up where we are headed.

Chinese proverb

To defend the Biobío River has been an honour. To be human voices for the river... After all, it is obvious – it is for survival, it is for the children, it is for love.

Juan Pablo Orrego (contemporary), Chilean indigenous rights activist and environmental campaigner

The people are starving. They need food; they need medicine; they need education. They do not need a skyscraper to house the ruling party and a 24-hour TV station.

Wangari Maathai (1940-), founder of the Green Belt Movement in Kenya who, in 2004, became the first African woman to receive the Nobel Peace Prize

The only two herbicides we recommend are cultivation and mulching.

Organic Gardening Magazine

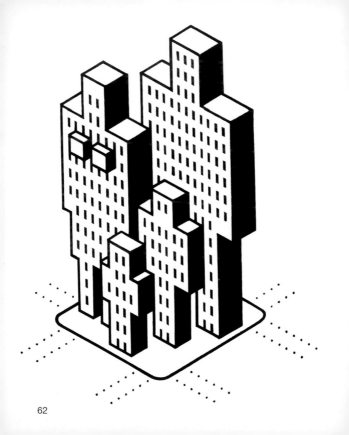

62

THE WAIT-AND-SEE OPTION IS NOT ON: THE LONGER WE WAIT, THE MORE UNLIKELY THE POSSIBILITY OF A SMOOTH TRANSITION TO SUSTAINABILITY BECOMES. THE CHALLENGE IS CLEAR AND THE ALTERNATIVES NOT VERY APPEALING. ECOLOGICAL INSTABILITY AND SOCIO-POLITICAL CHAOS ARE NOT WHAT I WANT FOR MY CHILDREN. HOW ABOUT YOU?

Wayne Ellwood (1949-), Canadian journalist

64

Thank god that men cannot fly, and lay waste the sky as well as earth.

Henry David Thoreau (1817-1862), writer/philosopher

Give a man a fish, and he can eat for a day, but teach a man how to fish...

...and he'll be dead of mercury poisoning inside of three years.

Charles N Haas
(contemporary), US
environmental engineer

Monsanto should not have to vouchsafe the safety of biotech food. Our interest is in selling as much of it as possible. Assuring its safety is the FDA's [US Food and Drug Administration] job.

Phil Angell (contemporary), Director of Corporate Communications of US biotech giant Monsanto

Only to the white man was nature a 'wilderness'.

Luther Standing Bear (1868-1939),
former Oglala Lakota Chief

The task ahead of us is never as great as the power behind us.

Ralph Waldo Emerson (1803-1882), essayist

73

[Telling people to plant trees to help the climate] is like telling people to drink more water to keep down rising sea-levels.

Oliver Rackham (contemporary),
British forest historian

"SURE I'D LIKE ANOTHER SHOT AT A LUNAR LANDING, GENERAL... JUST DON'T HAVE THE ACREAGE..."

Perhaps in the thousand ages of divine-like patience, even this rock of mindlessness will be dented by the regular dripping of roof water.

Chinua Achebe (1930-), Nigerian novelist

Opposition to nuclear energy is based on irrational fear fed by Hollywood-style fiction, the Green lobbies and the media.

James Lovelock (1919-), scientist and author famous for postulating the Gaia hypothesis which suggests that the Earth functions as a superorganism.

A young victim of the 1986 Chernobyl disaster – one of thousands of children born with severe birth defects due to over-exposure to radiation released from the nuclear reactor in Ukraine.

78

I'd put my money on the sun and solar energy. What a source of power! I hope we don't have to wait 'til oil and coal run out before we tackle that.

Thomas Alva Edison (1847-1931), US inventor

THE BOUNDLESS
BLUE SKY, THE
OCEAN WHICH
GIVES US BREATH
AND PROTECTS
US FROM THE
ENDLESS BLACK
AND DEATH,
IS BUT AN
INFINITESIMALLY
THIN FILM.

Vladimir Aleksandrovich Shatalov
(1927-), Russian Cosmonaut

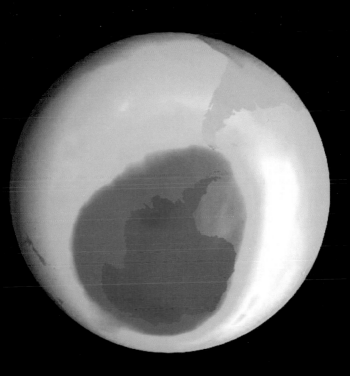

Satellite image of hole in the ozone layer exposing Antarctica.

THE UNIVERSE IS NOT
REQUIRED TO BE IN
PERFECT HARMONY
WITH HUMAN AMBITION.

The hardest task we face is not in stopping pollution and its causes, but in fighting the notion that a poisoned environment is 'normal' or 'inevitable'. Humans can get used to almost anything – and that is the greater danger.

Alan Hughes (1948-), British artist

The force that through the green fuse drives the flower, drives my green age.

Dylan Thomas (1914-1953), Welsh poet and writer.

Environmentalism, like almost everything else, is in danger of being swallowed by the corporate leviathan. If this happens, it will disappear without trace. No one threatens its survival as much as the greens who have taken the company shilling.

George Monbiot (contemporary), British journalist and writer

Science City amusement park, Kolkata, India.

The butcher relenteth not
at the bleating of the lamb;
neither is the heart of the cruel
moved with distress.

But the tears of the compassionate are sweeter than dew-drops, falling from roses on the bosom of spring.

Akhenaten, Egyptian pharaoh approximately 1375-1350 BCE

I am not one of those who shy away from protesting INJUSTICE and OPPRESSION, arguing that they are expected in a military regime. The MILITARY do not act alone. They are supported by a gaggle of politicians, lawyers, academics and businessmen, all of them HIDING under the claim that they are only DOING THEIR DUTY, men and women too afraid to wash their pants of urine.

Kenule Beeson Saro-Wiwa (1941-1995), Ogoni activist fighting against environmental destruction by oil companies (notably Shell) in the Niger Delta region. He was speaking at his trial just before his execution ordered by Nigerian dictator General Sani Abacha.

It's not easy being ...

EN!

Kermit the Frog, Muppet

Coca-Cola machine at the EDEN PROJECT in Cornwall, Britain.

Socialism collapsed because it did not allow the market to tell the *economic truth*. **Capitalism** may collapse because it does not allow the market to tell the *ecological truth*.

Øystein Dahle, former Vice President of Exxon for Norway and the North Sea

When the axe came into the forest, the trees said: 'The handle's one of us!'

Anonymous

It is an important and popular fact that things are not always how they seem. For instance, on the planet Earth, humans have always assumed that they were more intelligent than dolphins, because they had achieved so much – the wheel, New York, wars, and so on – whilst all the dolphins had ever done was muck about in the water having a good time. But conversely, the dolphins had always believed that they were far more intelligent than humans – for precisely the same reason.

Douglas Adams (1952-2001), British author

We've got to pause and ask ourselves: 'How much clean air do we need?'

Lee Iacocca (1924-), former CEO of Chrysler Corporation, reacting to Detroit's air pollution control proposals

Why, for instance, is a human-made phenomenon like global warming – which may kill hundreds of millions of human beings over the next century – considered 'environmental'? Why are poverty and war not considered environmental problems while global warming is? What are the implications of framing global warming as an environmental problem – and handing off the responsibility for dealing with it to 'environmentalists'?

Michael Shellenberger and Ted Nordhaus in 'The Death of Environmentalism', 2005

I am convinced that ecology can not be secret. Environmental openness is an inalienable human right. Any attempt to conceal any information about harmful impacts on people and environment is a crime against humanity.

Alexander Nikitin (contemporary), former Russian naval officer turned environmentalist. He has been harassed and imprisoned for revealing sources of radioactive contamination in the northwestern region of Russia.

I often say openly that if you are hard (*keras*) I will also be hard. But I say that because I work hard to defend myself and fight against violence towards women and other victims of men or outsiders in military uniforms or from the civil government or Freeport [McMoran]. Whoever they are... And I think that my attitude and my struggle represent the attitude and experience of women in Papua every day. I can't turn back now.

Yosepha Alomang (contemporary), West Papuan community leader talking about her simultaneous struggle aginst US mining company Freeport McMoran, the Indonesian military and patriarchal attitudes in her own community.

We are monumentally distracted by a pervasive technological culture that appears to have a life of its own, one that insists

on our full attention, continually seducing us and pulling us away from the opportunity to experience directly the true meaning of our own lives.

Al Gore, former US Vice-President and self-professed 'inventor' of the internet

Polyp

*Film star
Marilyn Monroe
pictured at
Idlewild airport,
New York,
1954.*

GET A FEEL FOR FUR: SLAM YOUR FINGERS IN A CAR DOOR.

Anonymous

All of our technical and scientific capacity will have to be used to reverse the process of destruction we have created. I am proud to be from Amazônia where we still have a chance to start a sustainable history.

Marina Silva (contemporary), Amazonian rubber tapper and community leader. She, together with Chico Mendes, helped form *empates* – peaceful grassroots actions by communities of rubber tappers to stop forest destruction and land evictions.

Native communities are focal points for the excrement of industrial society.

Winona La Duke (contemporary), Ojibwa (Minnesota, US) community organizer, economist and author

Young boy at Pine Ridge Reservation, South Dakota.

THE AUTOMOBILE has proved to be the single most environmentally destructive work of technology in history. Each gallon of gas burned releases 22 pounds of carbon dioxide into the atmosphere. In a year, the average car emits five tons of carbon dioxide into the air. With over 120 million automobiles in the United States, automobile emissions account for 33 per cent of all carbon dioxide and 45 percent of all nitrous oxide released into the sky, making the car the single largest contributor to global warming.

Jeremy Rifkin (1943-), US environmental economist

Think of bicycles as rideable art that can just about save the world.

Grant Petersen (contemporary), US author and bicycle builder

Sitting from left: Former World Bank President James Wolfensohn, Zimbabwe's President Robert Mugabe, Kenya's President Daniel Arap Moi, Tanzania's President Benjamin Mkapa. Standing from left are: Eritrea's President Isaias Afwerki, Malawi's President Bakili Muluzi, Botswana's President Festus Mogae.

Because African political leaders have delegated their economic planning to the International Monetary Fund and the World Bank... they no longer have the power to protect their citizens or environment from being exploited by the First World.

Fatima Jibrell (contemporary), Somali environmentalist

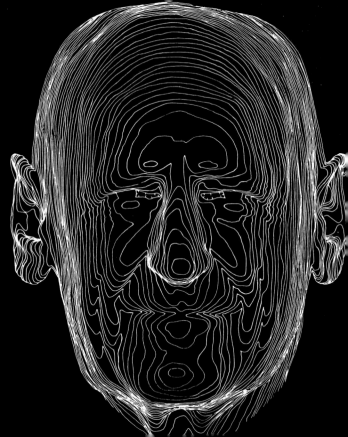

The human race is challenged more than ever before to demonstrate our mastery – not over nature but of ourselves.

Rachel Carson (1907-1964),
US biologist

Georgian & Azerbaijani dancers in the Abkhazia region.

Earth, people, and poetry are one and the same entity tied together by mysterious subterranean passages. When the earth blooms, the people breathe freedom, the poets sing and show the way.

Pablo Neruda (1904-1973), Chilean poet and winner of the Nobel Prize for Literature in 1971

We could have saved the Earth but we were too damned cheap.

Kurt Vonnegut (1922-), US author

DEVELOPMENT ISSUES cannot be contained within national boundaries. In India, even though there is hardly any land to relocate people onto, the projects are on the fast track, and those decisions are being made not just in Delhi and Bombay but also in Washington and Geneva. When there are more and more such projects going forward, the people's sovereignty over natural resources and human rights are bypassed. So it's essential that we reach the global centres of power to fight not just centralized planning, but privatization-based planning.

Medha Patkar, pictured right, (contemporary), Indian activist and community leader

... AS A SIGN OF MY TENDER LOVE FOR YOU, DARLING~FLOWERS GROWN IN AN IMPOVERISHED COUNTRY BY AN EXPLOITED WORKFORCE WHO'VE BEEN PAID STARVATION WAGES AND EXPOSED TO STERILITY-INDUCING PESTICIDES...

Each Valentine's Day, when US and other consumers purchase millions of flowers for their loved ones and deeply inhale the fresh aroma of roses and carnations, they rarely think about where the flowers come from or how they are produced. Yet, if these same people

knew more about the high levels of agrochemicals used in flower production and the often less-than-rosy labour conditions under which flowers are produced, they might think twice about sinking their noses into the petals to smell the perfume.

Environmental Health Perspectives, Vol 110, No 5, May 2002

Everything we do in this life requires proper action – even eating.

Pisit Charnsnoh (contemporary),
Thai marine conservationist

The automobile has not merely taken over the street, it has dissolved the living tissue of the city...

Gas-filled, noisy and hazardous, our streets have become the most inhumane landscape in the world.

James M Fitch (contemporary), US writer

Pulp mill, South Africa.

In the village, minus the timber companies, life is peaceful. No one says he owns this or that.

Harrison Ngau Laing (contemporary), Dayak Penan
indigenous community activist in Malaysia

MORE THAN AT ANY TIME IN HISTORY HUMANKIND FACES A CROSSROADS. ONE PATH LEADS TO DESPAIR AND UTTER HOPELESSNESS, THE OTHER TO TOTAL EXTINCTION. LET US PRAY THAT WE HAVE THE WISDOM TO CHOOSE CORRECTLY.

Woody Allen, (1935-), US filmmaker, writer and comedian

The frog does not drink up the pond in which it lives.

Chinese proverb

SATELLITE PICTURES OF THE EARTH SCANNING CROPS, PASTURES AND FORESTS EVOKE A SPURIOUS UNIVERSALISM. IN THESE PICTURES, HUMAN BEINGS AND WHAT NATURE MEANS TO THEM AND THEIR LIVES ARE MISSING. GLOBAL RESOURCE MANAGEMENT TENDS TO DISREGARD THE LOCAL CONTEXT. SUCH DISREGARD USED TO GO UNDER THE NAME OF COLONIALISM.

Wolfgang Sachs (contemporary), German writer and academic

AFTER 15 YEARS of structural adjustment, when we thought that the most important human values had been wrested from us, when we thought we were incapable of overcoming fear, of having the ability to organize and unite, when we no longer believed we could make our voices heard, then our humble, simple and hard-working people — men, women, children and the elderly — demonstrated to the country and to the world that all this is still posssible.

Oscar Olivera, Bolivian community leader talking about the successful struggle in Cochabamba against water privatization forced by World Bank and IMF loan conditionalities.

1 Carbon Cred

the value of the credit will go up and
according to global market speculat
and is at no time under any circumsta
in anyway related to any known con
of the ecological cost of industrial ac

to complete your carbon portfolio we recommend complementary investments in the futures carbon exchange ma

HISTORY HAS SEEN attempts to
commodify land, food, labour, forests,
water, genes and ideas. Carbon trading
follows in the footsteps of this history
and turns the earth's carbon-cycling
capacity into property to be bought or
sold in a global market...

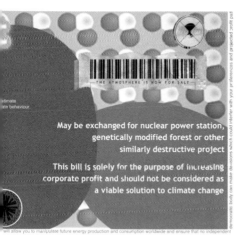

THE ATMOSPHERE IS NOW FOR SALE

May be exchanged for nuclear power station,
genetically modified forest or other
similarly destructive project

This bill is solely for the purpose of increasing
corporate profit and should not be considered as
a viable solution to climate change

'Giving carbon a price' will not prove to be any more effective, democratic, or conducive to human welfare, than giving genes, forests, biodiversity or clean rivers a price.

'Durban Declaration', 10 October 2004, signed by dozens of grassroots groups, NGOs and community organizations fighting climate change

Stars, hills, clouds, trees, birds, crickets, humans: each has its world, each is a world, and yet all of these worlds correspond. We can only defend life if we experience a revival of this feeling of solidarity with nature.

Octavio Paz (1914-1998), Mexican poet, writer and diplomat who won the Nobel Prize for Literature in 1990.

We are many people,
and we know
that this effort is
worthwhile not only
for ourselves but also
for the whole world.
If some of us have
to die, that means
that some of us have
to continue – and in
that persistence one
finds the strength for
the struggle.

Libia Grueso (contemporary),
Afro-Colombian civil rights and
environmental activist

153

East Moors Steelworks, Splott, Cardiff Bay, South Wales, 1972.

There's so much pollution in the air now that if it weren't for our lungs there'd be no place to put it all.

Robert Orben (1927-), US humourist and former speech writer for Richard Nixon and Gerald Ford

Lord, take my soul, but the struggle continues.

The last words of Kenule Beeson Saro-Wiwa (1941-1995), writer and leader of the Movement for the Survival of the Ogoni People. He was hanged along with eight other activists by the Nigerian military dictatorship on 10 November 1995. They had been campaigning against the environmental destruction of their homeland by oil companies, particularly Shell.

THE BALANCE goes to the leaves,
into the soil, into the water,
into all forms of wildlife, into
ourselves. What is good for
the balance sheet is wasteful of
resources and harmful to life.
When the planes still swoop

down and aerial spray a field in order to kill a predator insect with pesticides, we are in the Dark Ages of commerce. Maybe one thousandth of this aerial insecticide actually prevents the infestation.

Paul Hawken (contemporary), US environmentalist and entrepreneur

BLUE -GREEN ALGAE BL

HIGH CONCENTRATIONS OF BLUE-GREEN ALGAE HAVE BEEN FOUND IN

SWALLOWING THE WATER OR ALGAL SCUM CAN CAUSE STOMACH UPSETS C
HEALTH EFFECTS
CONTACT WITH THE WATER OR WITH ALGAL SCUM CAN CAUSE SKIN

IT IS A SENSIBLE PRECAUTION FOR YOU. YOUR CHILDREN AND YOUR ANIM
CONTACT WITH THE SCUM AND THE WATER CLOSE TO IT

8TH AUGUST 2003
OXFORD CITY COUNCIL

FOR FURTHER
TELEPHONE C

160

THE MAJOR public acceptance barrier which surfaced in all the case studies is the widely held perception of sewage sludge as malodorous, disease causing or otherwise repulsive... There is an irrational component to public attitudes about sludge which means that public education will not be entirely successful.

US Environment Protection Agency, 1981 public relations document as quoted in 'Toxic Sludge is Good for You: Lies, Damned Lies, and the Public Relations Industry' by John Stauber and Sheldon Rampton, Common Courage Press, 1995.

OMS

WATER

ORE SERIOUS

LEMS

TO AVOID

FORMATION
5 252486

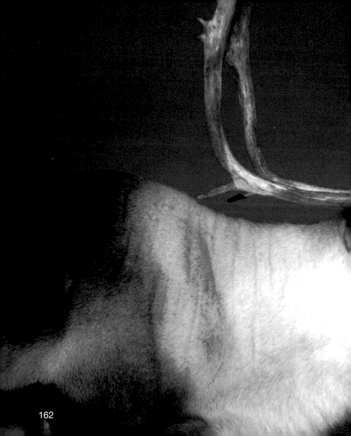

162

We are caribou people. It's our clothing, our story, our song, our dance and our food that's who we are. If you drill for oil here, you are drilling right into the heart of our existence.

Sarah James
(contemporary),
Gwichíin (Alaska)
community leader
fighting against the
Bush Administration's
efforts to drill for oil in the
Alaska National Wildlife Refuge
which threatens migrating herds of caribou
and the people that depend on them.

163

We need to gather together all the litterers... and throw them away.

Anonymous

We're creating a sort of 'climate apartheid', wherein the poorest and darkest-skinned pay the highest price – with their health, their land, and, in some cases, with their lives – for continued carbon profligacy by the rich.

Soumitra Ghosh (contemporary), National Forum of Forest Peoples and Forest Workers in India criticizing the corporate-backed trade in 'rights to pollute' as enshrined in the Kyoto climate treaty.

MEMO

Just between you and me, shouldn't the World Bank be encouraging more migration of the dirty industries to the LDCs [Least Developed Countries]? ...the economic logic behind dumping a load of toxic waste in the lowest wage country is impeccable, and we should face up to that... I've always thought that under-populated countries in Africa are vastly underpolluted; their air quality is probably vastly inefficiently low compared to Los Angeles or Mexico City...The concern over an agent that causes a one-in-a-million change in the odds of prostate cancer is obviously going to be much higher in a country where people survive to get prostate cancer than in a country where under-five mortality is 200 per thousand.

Lawrence Summers (1954-), former World Bank Chief Economist who later became US Treasury Secretary and is currently President of Harvard University

170

By destroying our forests, our trees, our wild animals, and our rivers, the Burmese dictatorship and its partners in crime also destroy who we are. Even though they have the money, guns and power, we have truth and justice on our side to defend human rights and the environment.

Ka Hsaw Wa, pictured left, (contemporary), Burmese human rights activist and co-founder of Earth Rights International

'Shantytown' adjacent to oil refinery in Durban, South Africa.

Communities must not relent in their struggle against environmental injustices and racism, and should not let the obstacles of industrial and state power foil their quest for the ideal environment.

Bobby Peek (contemporary),
South African environmental
justice campaigner

173

Before you finish eating breakfast this morning, you've depended on more than half the world. This is the way our universe is structured. We aren't going to have peace on earth until we recognize this basic fact of the interrelated structure of reality.

Martin Luther King (1929-1968), US civil rights leader

Roma child playing near a factory in the polluted industrial town of Copsa Mica, Romania.

THE ROOTS of environmental injustice directly reflect inequalities in power. It's easier to locate and maintain highly polluting enterprises in communities that are without power.

Michael Belliveau (contemporary), US environmental justice activist as quoted in the documentary 'Green Gold', 2002.

The smoke caught us. We tried opening our eyes in the morning, but we couldn't open them. Our eyes were sore, red and shut.

Eileen Kampakuta Brown, pictured left, (contemporary), Aboriginal elder describing the effects of fallout from British nuclear testing in South Australia where Aboriginal people were housed in unsafe shelters and assured that the testing was harmless to them.

here's to our last drink of fossil fuels
let us vow to get off of this sauce
shoo away the swarms of commuter planes
and find that train ticket we lost
cuz once upon a time the line followed
the river
and peeked into all the backyards
and the laundry was waving
the graffiti was teasing us
from brick walls and bridges
we were rolling over ridges
through valleys
under stars
i dream of touring like duke ellington
in my own railroad car
i dream of waiting on the tall blonde wooden
benches
in a grand station aglow with grace
and then standing out on the platform
and feeling the air on my face

ani difranco (1970-), US singer/songwriter,
from her poem 'self evident'

Oil refineries and chemical plants a stone's throw from a residential estate in Grangemouth, Scotland.

When we talk about climate change, it must be in the context of social justice. If we deal with it only as an 'environmental' problem, we are likely to reinforce an economic and political system that exacerbates the unequal relations between the peoples of the world. It is for this reason that we must demand climate justice.

Heidi Bachram (1972-), British environmental justice campaigner and documentary filmmaker

UN Secretary-General Kofi Annan giving a keynote speech to participants of a controversial corporate lobbying event at the World Summit for Sustainable Development in Johannesburg, South Africa 2002.

I'm only a child and I don't have all the solutions, but I want you to realize, NEITHER DO YOU! You don't know how to fix the holes in the ozone layer. You don't know how to bring the salmon back up a dead stream. You don't know how to bring back an animal now extinct. And you can't bring back a forest where there is now a desert. If you don't know how to fix it, PLEASE STOP BREAKING IT!

Severn Cullis-Suzuki, age 12 speaking to delegates at the original Earth Summit, Rio de Janeiro, Brazil, June 1992.

ORGANIZATIONS

Just some of the many campaigning organizations whose environmental activism has a strong element of human rights and social justice. Most organizations listed here are engaged in international activities.

Action Group on Erosion, Technology and Concentration
1 Gilmour St, Second Floor,
Ottawa, ON, K2P 0R5
CANADA
tel: +1 613 241 2267
www.etcgroup.org

Aid Watch
19 Eve St Erskineville NSW
2043 AUSTRALIA
tel: +61 (0) 2 9557 8944
aidwatch@aidwatch.org.au
www.aidwatch.org.au

Black Environment Network
1st Floor, 60 High Street
Llanberis, Wales, LL55 4EU
BRITAIN
tel/fax: +44 (0)1286 870715
ukoffice@ben-network.org.uk
www.ben-network.org.uk

Carbon Trade Watch
Transnational Institute
Paulus Potterstraat 20
1071 DA Amsterdam
NETHERLANDS
tel: +31 20 662 6608
info@carbontradewatch.org
www.carbontradewatch.org

Centre for Science and the Environment
41, Tughlakabad Institutional
Area, New Delhi-110062
INDIA
tel: +91 (0)11 299 55124
cse@cseindia.org
www.cseindia.org

The Corner House
Station Road, Sturminster
Newton, Dorset DT10 1YJ
BRITAIN
tel: +44 (0)1258 473 795

enquiries@thecornerhouse.org.uk
www.thecornerhouse.org.uk

Corporate Europe Observatory
Paulus Potterstraat 20
1071 DA Amsterdam
NETHERLANDS
tel/fax: +31 20 612 7023
ceo@corporateeurope.org
www.corporateeurope.org

Corporate Watch
16b Cherwell St., Oxford
OX4 1BG, BRITAIN
tel: +44 (0)1865 791 391
mail@corporatewatch.org
www.corporatewatch.org

Corpwatch
1611 Telegraph Avenue, #702
Oakland, CA 94612
UNITED STATES
tel: 11 510 271 8080
info@corpwatch.org
www.corpwatch.org

Earth Rights International
1612 K St. NW, Suite 401,
Washington, DC 20006
UNITED STATES

tel: +1 202 466 5188
infousa@earthrights.org
www.earthrights.org

ECA Watch
www.eca-watch.org

Friends of the Earth Int'l
PO Box 19199, 1000 GD
Amsterdam, NETHERLANDS
tel: +31 20 622 1369
foei@foei.org
www.foei.org

Global Justice Ecology Project
PO Box 412, Hinesburg, VT
05461, UNITED STATES
tel: +1 802 482 2689
info@globaljusticeecology.org
www.globaljusticeecology.org

GRAIN
Girona 25, pral., E-08010,
Barcelona, SPAIN
tel: +34 93 301 1381
grain@grain.org
www.grain.org

IFI Watch Net
www.ifiwatchnet.org

Indigenous Environment Network
PO Box 485, Bemidji, MN
56619 UNITED STATES
tel: +1 218 751 4967
ien@igc.org
www.ienearth.org

International Rivers Network
1847 Berkeley Way
Berkeley, CA 94703
UNITED STATES
tel: +1 510 848 1155
info@irn.org
www.irn.org

Oilwatch
Casilla 17-15-24-C,
Quito,
ECUADOR
www.oilwatch.org.ec

People for the Ethical Treatment of Animals (PETA)
501 Front St., Norfolk, VA
23510, UNITED STATES
tel: +1 757 622 PETA (7382)
info@peta.org
www.peta.org

Polaris Institute
312 Cooper Street
Ottawa ON, K2P 0G7
CANADA
tel: +1 613 237 1717
polaris@polarisinstitute.org
www.polarisinstitute.org

Probe International
225 Brunswick Avenue,
Toronto, Ontario M5S 2M6
CANADA
tel: +1 416 964 9223 ext. 100
www.probeinternational.org

Project Underground
1611 Telegraph Avenue, Suite
702, Oakland, CA 94612
UNITED STATES
tel: +1 510 271 8081
project_underground@moles.org
www.moles.org

Risingtide UK
62 Fieldgate Street
London E1 1ES, BRITAIN
info@risingtide.org.uk
www.risingtide.org.uk

Risingtide Aotearoa/ NZ
PO Box 7523, Wellesley Street,

Auckland,
NEW ZEALAND / AOTEAROA
contact@risingtide.org.nz
www.risingtide.org.nz

**Sustainable Energy and
Economy Network**
733-15th St., NW, Suite 1020
Washington, DC 20005
UNITED STATES
tel: +1 202 234 9382, ext.208
seen@seen.org
www.seen.org

Third World Network
121-S, Jalan Utama, 10450
Penang,
MALAYSIA
tel: +60 4 226 6728
twnet@po.jaring.my
www.twnside.org.sg

The Vegan Society
Donald Watson House, 7
Battle Road, St Leonards-on-
Sea, TN37 7AA,
BRITAIN
tel: +44 (0)1424 427 393
info@vegansociety.com
www.vegansociety.com

**Women's Environmental
Network**
PO Box 30626 London E1 1TZ
BRITAIN
tel: +44 (0)20 7481 9004
info@wen.org.uk
www.wen.org.uk

**World Development
Movement**
25 Beehive Place,
London, SW9 7QR BRITAIN
tel: +44 (0)20 7737 6215
wdm@wdm.org.uk
www.wdm.org.uk

**World Information Service
on Energy**
PO Box 59636
1040 LC Amsterdam
NETHERLANDS
tel: +31 20 612 6368
wiseamster@antenna.nl
www.antenna.nl/wise/

World Rainforest Movement
Maldonado 1858, 11200
Montevideo, URUGUAY
tel: +598 2 413 2989
wrm@wrm.org.uy
www.wrm.org.uy

New Internationalist Publications is a co-operative with offices in Oxford (England), Adelaide (Australia), Toronto (Canada) and Christchurch (New Zealand/Aotearoa). It exists to report on the issues of world poverty and inequality; to focus attention on the unjust relationship between the powerful and powerless in both rich and poor nations; to debate and campaign for the radical changes necessary within and between those nations if the basic material and spiritual needs of all are to be met; and to bring to life the people, the ideas, the action in the fight for global justice.

The monthly **New Internationalist** magazine now has more than 75,000 subscribers worldwide. In addition to the magazine, the co-operative publishes the One World Calendar and the One World Almanac, outstanding collections of full-colour photographs. It also publishes books, including: the successful series of No-Nonsense Guides to the key issues in the world today; cookbooks containing recipes and cultural information from around the world; and photographic books on topics such as Nomadic Peoples and Water. The **NI** is the English-language publisher of the biennial reference book *The World Guide*, written by the Instituto del Tercer Mundo in Uruguay.

The co-operative is financially independent but aims to break even; any surpluses are reinvested so as to bring New Internationalist publications to as many people as possible.

www.newint.org